AMAZING PICTURE PUZZLES

MORE THAN 200 VISUAL CHALLENGES!

THUNDER BAY
P·R·E·S·S
San Diego, California

Thunder Bay Press
An imprint of Printers Row Publishing Group
10350 Barnes Canyon Road, Suite 100, San Diego, CA 92121
www.thunderbaybooks.com

Thunder Bay Press
Publisher: Peter Norton
Publishing Team: Lori Asbury, Ana Parker, Laura Vignale, Kathryn Chipinka
Editorial Team: JoAnn Padgett, Melinda Allman, Dan Mansfield, Traci Douglas
Production Team: Jonathan Lopes, Rusty von Dyl, Susan Engbring

Cover design by Susan Engbring

Amazing Picture Puzzles
ISBN: 978-1-62686-797-0

Printed in China
20 19 18 17 16   1 2 3 4 5

Contents

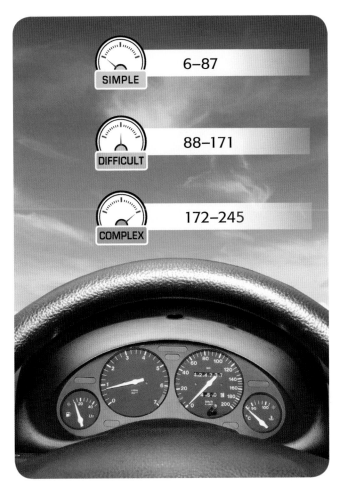

SPOT THE USAGE

Types of Puzzles

This book has three types of puzzles with one, two, or eight pictures on every page. Each puzzle may have five to ten differences, or an odd image that you have to spot.

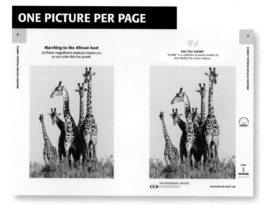

Compare the pictures on two opposite pages and spot the differences between them.

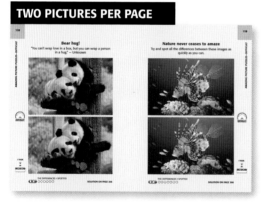

Compare two pictures on the same page and spot the differences between them.

Look at all eight pictures on the same page and spot the odd one out.

Symbols Used

1

Tick off one circle for every difference you find.

2

DID YOU KNOW?
Studies have proved that happy people live longer, make more money, and receive better job reviews.

The "Did You Know?" facts keep you interested as you go about spotting the differences!

3 | SOLUTION ON PAGE |

Help is close at hand. Just turn to the correct page to see the answers.

4

Record the time you take to find all the differences.

Difficulty meters

The sections are color coded to be in line with the difficulty meter. This is helpful in identifying the level of complexity of each puzzle. See how far you can push yourself!

SIMPLE   DIFFICULT   COMPLEX

Marching to the African beat

Let these magnificent creatures inspire you
as you solve this fun puzzle.

DID YOU KNOW?
"Giraffe" is a collection of poems written by
Don Mulford for senior citizens.

SIMPLE

I TOOK

MIN : SEC

THE DIFFERENCES I SPOTTED

SOLUTION ON PAGE 248

Pretty day, pretty me

On this perfect day, try and locate the one image that is odd.

SIMPLE

I TOOK

MIN : SEC

SOLUTION ON PAGE 248

Let's go diving!

Don't hold your breath, try and find the odd one out.

SIMPLE

I TOOK

MIN : SEC

SOLUTION ON PAGE 248

Zoom!

The Sydney Monorail connects Darling Harbour and Chinatown with the business and shopping districts of the city.

SIMPLE

I TOOK

MIN : SEC

THE DIFFERENCES I SPOTTED

 ○○○○○○○○○

SOLUTION ON PAGE 248

All the queen's men

In London, the Changing of the Guard is a formal ceremony
that occurs every time sentries are relieved of their duties.

SIMPLE

I TOOK

⏳

MIN : SEC

THE DIFFERENCES I SPOTTED

07 ○○○○○○○

SOLUTION ON PAGE 248

Best view in the house

These images may seem as though they have the same view, but there are many differences. Try and spot all ten of them.

SIMPLE

I TOOK

MIN : SEC

THE DIFFERENCES I SPOTTED

10 ○○○○○○○○○○

SOLUTION ON PAGE 248

Because she cares

"God could not be everywhere and therefore he made mothers."
— Unknown

SIMPLE

I TOOK

MIN : SEC

THE DIFFERENCES I SPOTTED

05 ⊕ ○○○○○

SOLUTION ON PAGE 249

Row, row, row your boat

Can you find all the differences between these two images?

SIMPLE

I TOOK

MIN : SEC

THE DIFFERENCES I SPOTTED

06 ○○○○○○

SOLUTION ON PAGE 249

You take my breath away

To bring good fortune, Buddhist prayer flags are strung between mountains all over Ladakh and other parts of the Himalayas.

SIMPLE

I TOOK

MIN : SEC

THE DIFFERENCES I SPOTTED

08

SOLUTION ON PAGE 249

Dance of the sails

Make the game even more exciting. Invite a friend to solve this puzzle with you and see who can spot the most differences.

SIMPLE

I TOOK

MIN : SEC

THE DIFFERENCES I SPOTTED

09 ○○○○○○○○○

SOLUTION ON PAGE 249

Picture postcard

These houses are not quite picture perfect.
Can you spot the differences?

SIMPLE

I TOOK

MIN : SEC

THE DIFFERENCES I SPOTTED

06

SOLUTION ON PAGE 249

Wide-eyed and watching

If you look carefully, you will be able to find all the differences between these two images.

DID YOU KNOW?
The average life span of a ring-tailed lemur is 18 years in the wild and 25 years in captivity.

SIMPLE

I TOOK

MIN : SEC

THE DIFFERENCES I SPOTTED

06 ○○○○○○

SOLUTION ON PAGE 249

Let's dance all night!

Before the concert ends, try and spot the odd image.

SIMPLE

I TOOK

MIN : SEC

SOLUTION ON PAGE 250

Dancing to my own beat

The Sun Dance is a religious ceremony performed by several Native American communities and tribes such as the Arapaho and Ute.

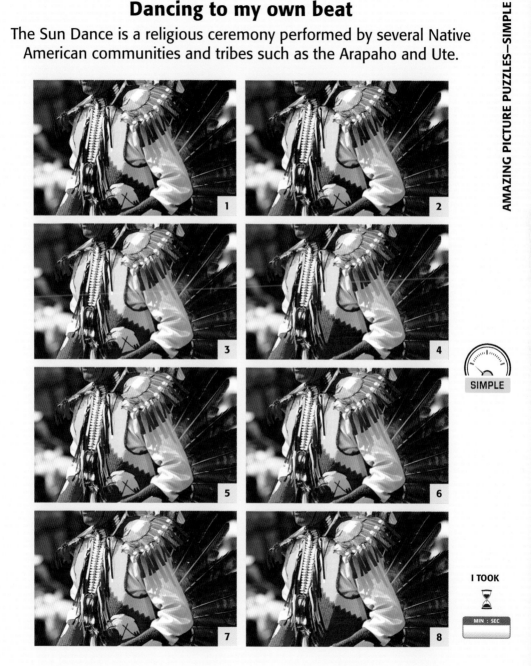

SIMPLE

I TOOK

MIN : SEC

SOLUTION ON PAGE 250

AMAZING PICTURE PUZZLES—SIMPLE

From Munich with love
Try and find the image that is unlike the others.

SIMPLE

I TOOK

MIN : SEC

SOLUTION ON PAGE 250

Pretty creative

Park Guell is an architectural garden complex in Barcelona, designed by Antoni Gaudi.

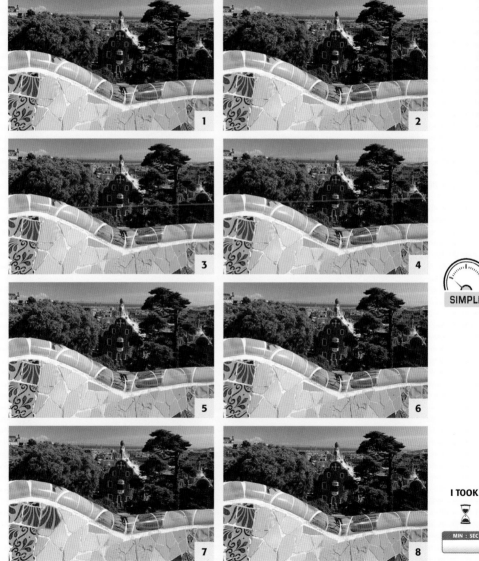

SIMPLE

I TOOK

MIN : SEC

SOLUTION ON PAGE 250

Leap of faith

Horse jumping was popularized by the English in the eighteenth century, when they had to jump fences on their fox hunts.

SIMPLE

I TOOK

MIN : SEC

THE DIFFERENCES I SPOTTED

08

SOLUTION ON PAGE 250

A tub of puppies

Add to the fun. Solve this puzzle against the clock.

SIMPLE

I TOOK

MIN : SEC

THE DIFFERENCES I SPOTTED

06 ○○○○○○

SOLUTION ON PAGE 250

Yin and yang

Restore the balance by finding all the differences
between the images.

SIMPLE

I TOOK

MIN : SEC

Catch of the day!

"Noodling" is when one catches the catfish with their bare hands. Do you think you can catch all the differences between the two images?

SIMPLE

I TOOK

MIN : SEC

THE DIFFERENCES I SPOTTED

08

SOLUTION ON PAGE 251

Twins to marvel at

The Petronas Towers are the tallest twin towers in the world,
and are located in Kuala Lumpur, Malaysia.

DID YOU KNOW?

The Petronas Twin Towers were the tallest buildings in the world until 2004, when Taipei 101 was completed. Even taller, the Burj Khalifa, built in Dubai in 2010, stands at 2,717 feet.

SIMPLE

I TOOK

MIN : SEC

THE DIFFERENCES I SPOTTED

09 ○○○○○○○○○

SOLUTION ON PAGE 251

The king of camouflage

There are approximately 160 species of chameleons throughout the world –from Hawaii in America, to Sri Lanka in Asia, to Madagascar in Africa.

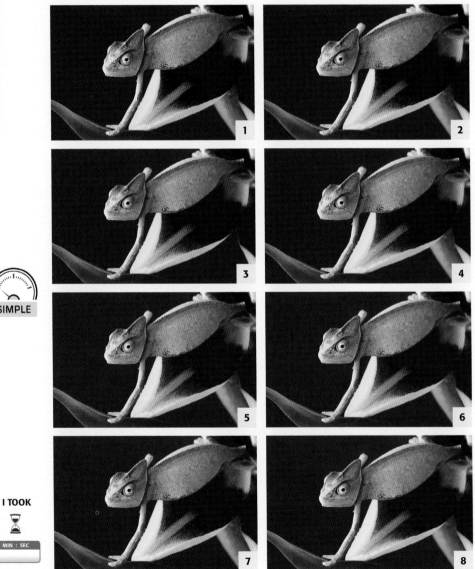

SIMPLE

I TOOK

MIN : SEC

SOLUTION ON PAGE 251

An exotic couple

All these colorful images may look the same, but there is an odd one. Try and spot it.

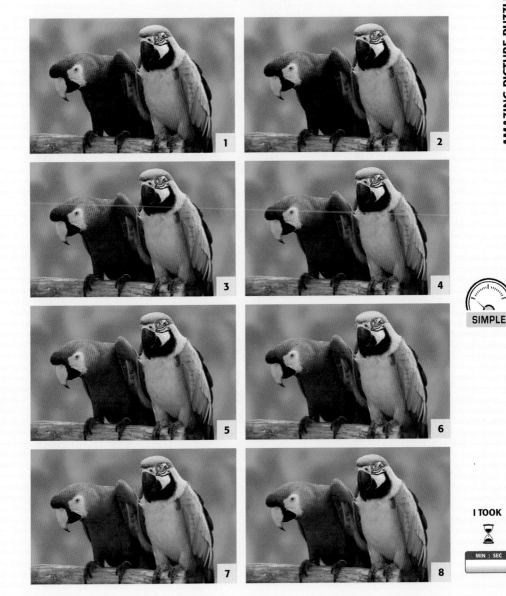

SIMPLE

I TOOK

MIN : SEC

SOLUTION ON PAGE 251

Questioning authority

You may be able to answer their questions by spotting all the differences between the two images.

SIMPLE

I TOOK

MIN : SEC

THE DIFFERENCES I SPOTTED

SOLUTION ON PAGE 251

Afloat with happiness

Try and find all the differences between these two family portraits.

SIMPLE

I TOOK

MIN : SEC

THE DIFFERENCES I SPOTTED

07

SOLUTION ON PAGE 252

It's not about the bike

Tuk-tuk racing is very popular in Thailand as well as in other Asian countries, including India and Vietnam.

SIMPLE

I TOOK

MIN : SEC

THE DIFFERENCES I SPOTTED

07 ⏱ ○○○○○○○

SOLUTION ON PAGE 252

Our red telephone booth

The red telephone booth was designed by
Sir Giles Gilbert Scott in the 1920s.

SIMPLE

I TOOK

MIN : SEC

THE DIFFERENCES I SPOTTED

06

SOLUTION ON PAGE 252

When passion and power collide

It is the mare that plays the role of leader in the herd, and she is often referred to as the "boss mare."

SIMPLE

I TOOK

MIN : SEC

THE DIFFERENCES I SPOTTED

SOLUTION ON PAGE 252

This print suits me best

The cheetah is one of the four cats that has semiretractable claws.
The others are the fishing cat, flat-headed cat, and Iriomote cat.

SIMPLE

I TOOK

MIN : SEC

THE DIFFERENCES I SPOTTED

06 ○○○○○○

SOLUTION ON PAGE 252

The baby munch bunch

Without getting too distracted by all the cuteness, try and locate all the differences between the images.

SIMPLE

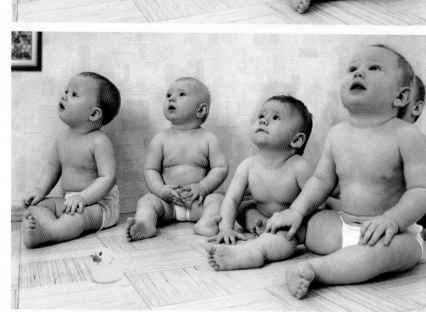

I TOOK

MIN : SEC

THE DIFFERENCES I SPOTTED

05 ○○○○○

SOLUTION ON PAGE 252

My world, my friends

"A friend is one who knows you and loves you just the same."
— Elbert Hubbard

SIMPLE

I TOOK

MIN : SEC

THE DIFFERENCES I SPOTTED

08 ○○○○○○○○

SOLUTION ON PAGE 253

Now that's a room with a view!

The Singapore Flyer is one of the tallest Ferris wheels in the world, standing 541 feet high.

SIMPLE

I TOOK

MIN : SEC

THE DIFFERENCES I SPOTTED

08 ○○○○○○○○

SOLUTION ON PAGE 253

Always color in my life

In Argentina, it is very common among the locals to paint their houses colorfully. This is most prominent in Buenos Aires.

SIMPLE

I TOOK

MIN : SEC

THE DIFFERENCES I SPOTTED

SOLUTION ON PAGE 253

Let's see what's out there

Solve this pretty puzzle as quickly as possible and beat the clock!

SIMPLE

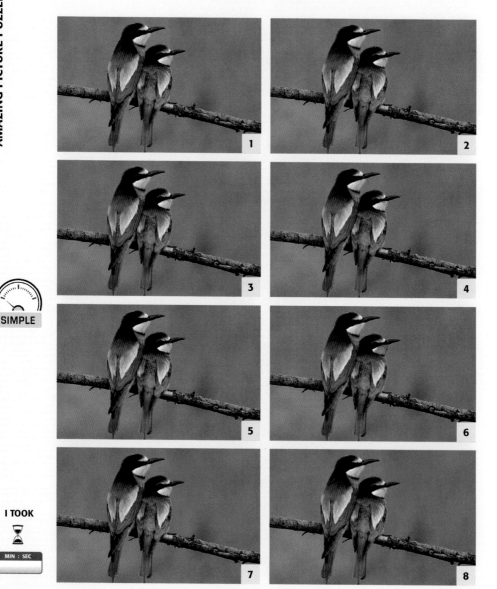

I TOOK

MIN : SEC

SOLUTION ON PAGE 253

The power of love

"Soul meets soul on lovers' lips."
— Percy Bysshe Shelley

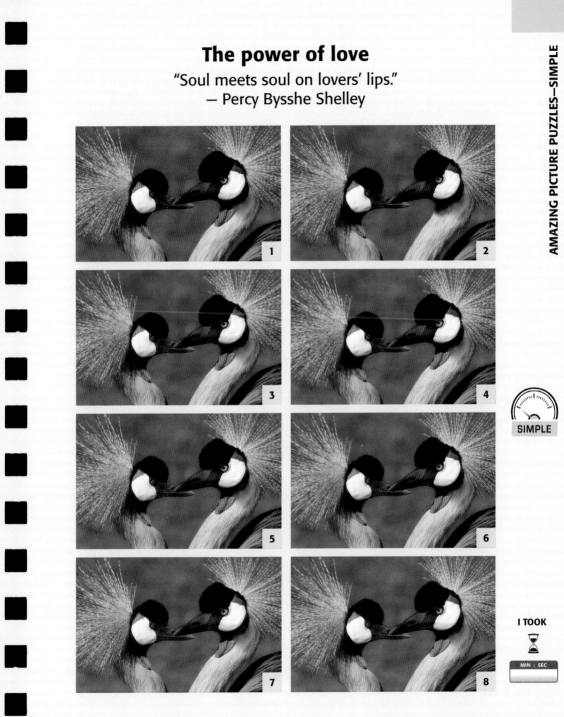

SIMPLE

I TOOK

MIN : SEC

SOLUTION ON PAGE 253

Travel fun!
"Celebrate the happiness that friends are always giving,
make every day a holiday and celebrate just living!"
— Amanda Bradley

DID YOU KNOW?
Greece's mainland, as well as the quaint islands that surround it, have many historical sites that one feels like revisiting again and again.

SIMPLE

I TOOK

MIN : SEC

THE DIFFERENCES I SPOTTED

09 ○○○○○○○○○

SOLUTION ON PAGE 253

Uniquely holy

Built in the 17th century, Novodevichy Convent was proclaimed a World Heritage Site by UNESCO in 2004.

SIMPLE

I TOOK

MIN : SEC

THE DIFFERENCES I SPOTTED

08 ○○○○○○○○○

SOLUTION ON PAGE 254

City icon

Finding all the differences between these two images is a lot simpler than finding a yellow cab in New York City during peak hours.

SIMPLE

I TOOK

MIN : SEC

THE DIFFERENCES I SPOTTED

07 ○○○○○○○

SOLUTION ON PAGE 254

My koala

These cute tree-hugging marsupials are solitary animals,
and therefore are never found in packs.

SIMPLE

I TOOK

MIN : SEC

THE DIFFERENCES I SPOTTED

05 ⬧ ○○○○○

SOLUTION ON PAGE 254

Hanging around

Leopards are solitary animals. They are seldom seen interacting apart from mating or rearing their young.

SIMPLE

I TOOK

MIN : SEC

THE DIFFERENCES I SPOTTED

07

SOLUTION ON PAGE 254

Color in my step. Color in my life.
As dazzling as her outfit is, can you locate the odd image?

SIMPLE

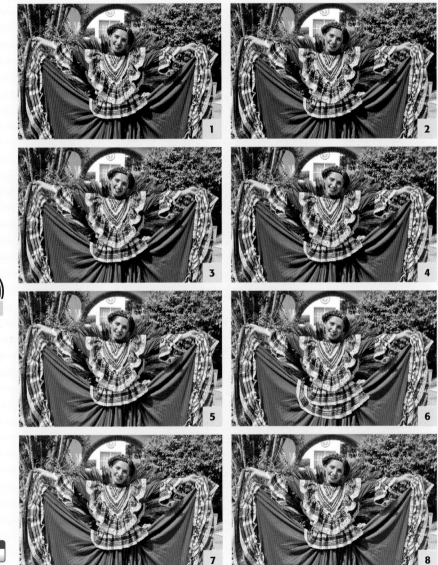

I TOOK

MIN : SEC

SOLUTION ON PAGE 254

Geronimo!
Spot the odd image.

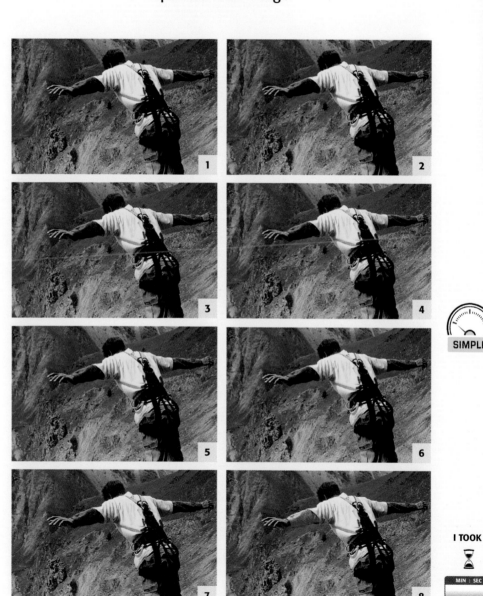

SIMPLE

I TOOK

MIN : SEC

SOLUTION ON PAGE 254

I bring the color to my life

After a nice walk, sit back and enjoy solving this fun puzzle.

SIMPLE

I TOOK

MIN : SEC

THE DIFFERENCES I SPOTTED

07

SOLUTION ON PAGE 255

A palace of dreams

Morocco is famous for its palatial architecture. See if you can spot all the differences between the two images.

SIMPLE

I TOOK

MIN : SEC

THE DIFFERENCES I SPOTTED

08 ○○○○○○○○

SOLUTION ON PAGE 255

Our favorite watering hole

Taking inspiration from these wise, gentle giants, see if you can find all the differences between these two images.

SIMPLE

I TOOK

MIN : SEC

THE DIFFERENCES I SPOTTED

SOLUTION ON PAGE 255

Some picnic fun
Try and solve this puzzle before the round is over.

SIMPLE

I TOOK

MIN : SEC

THE DIFFERENCES I SPOTTED

SOLUTION ON PAGE 255

No snow angel here

One is never too old for games, especially snowball fights.
Try and spot all the differences as quickly as possible.

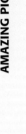

SIMPLE

I TOOK

MIN : SEC

THE DIFFERENCES I SPOTTED

08 ○○○○○○○○

SOLUTION ON PAGE 255

Hop, skip, jump, let's shop!

The Mall of America opened in 1992 in Bloomington, Minnesota. It is the largest mall in the United States.

SIMPLE

I TOOK

MIN : SEC

THE DIFFERENCES I SPOTTED

07

SOLUTION ON PAGE 255

Bangkok's mascots

The Thai rickshaw or bicycle taxi is known as a *samlor* in Thai.

SIMPLE

I TOOK

MIN : SEC

THE DIFFERENCES I SPOTTED

07 ○○○○○○○

SOLUTION ON PAGE 256

Docked

Puerto Madero in Buenos Aires is a very popular tourist destination, especially among those who enjoy sailing.

SIMPLE

I TOOK

MIN : SEC

THE DIFFERENCES I SPOTTED

06 ○○○○○○

SOLUTION ON PAGE 256

My home goes where I go

"Mediterranean tortoise" is the common name for a group of tortoises that includes the spur-thighed tortoise and the Hermann's tortoise.

SIMPLE

I TOOK

MIN : SEC

SOLUTION ON PAGE 256

Aflame with color

The life expectancy of flamingoes is one of the longest in birds, as they can live up to the age of forty.

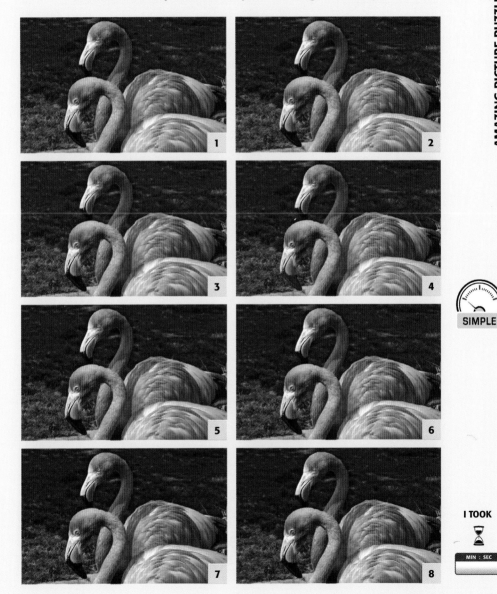

SIMPLE

I TOOK

MIN : SEC

Up and away!

"Imagination is the highest kite one can fly."
— Lauren Bacall

DID YOU KNOW?

In 1752, Benjamin Franklin flew a kite in a thunderstorm that resulted in him proving that lightning is a natural phenomenon and not a supernatural one.

SIMPLE

I TOOK

MIN : SEC

THE DIFFERENCES I SPOTTED

SOLUTION ON PAGE 256

A park for dreamers

Central Park in New York was proclaimed a
National Historic Landmark in 1963.

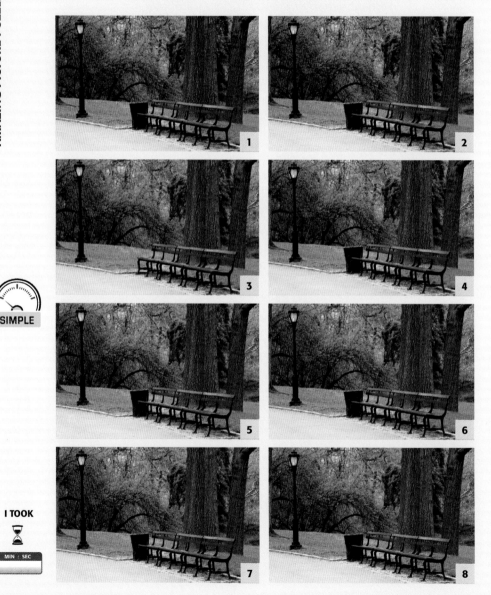

SIMPLE

I TOOK

MIN : SEC

SOLUTION ON PAGE 256

The Golden Gate Bridge

The Golden Gate Bridge was the longest suspension bridge in the world at the time of its completion in 1937.

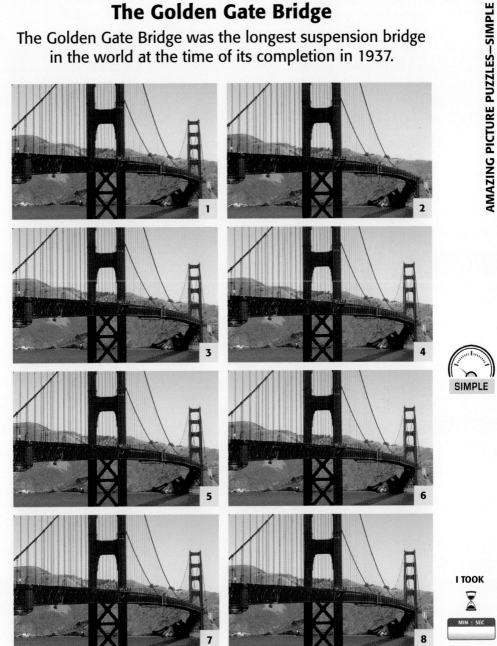

SIMPLE

I TOOK

MIN : SEC

SOLUTION ON PAGE 257

Happy as a duck in water

"Be like a duck. Calm on the surface, but always paddling like the dickens underneath." — Michael Caine

SIMPLE

I TOOK

MIN : SEC

THE DIFFERENCES I SPOTTED

SOLUTION ON PAGE 257

Family picnic

"A happy family is but an earlier heaven." — John Bowring

SIMPLE

I TOOK

⏳

MIN : SEC

THE DIFFERENCES I SPOTTED

06 ○○○○○○

SOLUTION ON PAGE 257

Hats of fun

The first rimmed hat was called the Phrygian cap, worn by freed Greek and Roman slaves in the early sixteenth century.

SIMPLE

I TOOK

MIN : SEC

THE DIFFERENCES I SPOTTED

05 ○○○○○

SOLUTION ON PAGE 257

Engineering the future

The first "skyscraper" was Chicago's Home Insurance Building, constructed in 1885. It was ten stories tall.

SIMPLE

I TOOK

MIN : SEC

THE DIFFERENCES I SPOTTED

08 ○○○○○○○○○

SOLUTION ON PAGE 257

Oh Marrakech!

Marrakech is the fourth-largest city in Morocco after Casablanca, Rabat, and Fez.

SIMPLE

I TOOK

MIN : SEC

THE DIFFERENCES I SPOTTED

SOLUTION ON PAGE 257

Pretty in blue

Chefchaouen is located in the Rif Mountains in Morocco.
The city is known for its beautiful blue buildings.

SIMPLE

I TOOK

MIN : SEC

THE DIFFERENCES I SPOTTED

06 ○○○○○○

SOLUTION ON PAGE 258

The funniest caravan

The camels that are found in India have a single hump.

SIMPLE

I TOOK

MIN : SEC

THE DIFFERENCES I SPOTTED

07 ○○○○○○○

SOLUTION ON PAGE 258

Thanksgiving
Thanksgiving has been observed in the United States since 1863.

SIMPLE

I TOOK

MIN : SEC

THE DIFFERENCES I SPOTTED

06 ○○○○○○

SOLUTION ON PAGE 258

Shape up!

It's a weighing issue. Can you spot the odd image?

SIMPLE

I TOOK

MIN : SEC

SOLUTION ON PAGE 258

Discovery unbound

There are plenty of discoveries but only one odd image.
Can you find it?

SIMPLE

I TOOK

MIN : SEC

SOLUTION ON PAGE 258

Beauty across the bridge

The Mausoleum of Hadrian, a cylindrically structured museum, was built by the Roman emperor Hadrian for him and his family.

SIMPLE

I TOOK

MIN : SEC

THE DIFFERENCES I SPOTTED

07 ○○○○○○○

SOLUTION ON PAGE 258

A pose just for you

"Honeymoon: a short period of doting between dating and debating." — Ray Bandy

SIMPLE

I TOOK

MIN : SEC

THE DIFFERENCES I SPOTTED

08 ○○○○○○○○

SOLUTION ON PAGE 259

Wild cat

The Bengal tiger is the largest tiger subspecies,
second only to the Siberian tiger.

SIMPLE

I TOOK

MIN : SEC

THE DIFFERENCES I SPOTTED

 07

SOLUTION ON PAGE 259

Home is where I go

The Chinese consider the turtle to symbolize wisdom
and patience.

SIMPLE

I TOOK

MIN : SEC

THE DIFFERENCES I SPOTTED

07 ○○○○○○○

SOLUTION ON PAGE 259

Riot police

Try and locate all the differences between the two images.

SIMPLE

I TOOK

MIN : SEC

THE DIFFERENCES I SPOTTED

09 ○○○○○○○○○

SOLUTION ON PAGE 259

New kids on the block

To date, Britain's most successful boy band has been One Direction.

SIMPLE

I TOOK

MIN : SEC

THE DIFFERENCES I SPOTTED

06 ○○○○○○

SOLUTION ON PAGE 259

AMAZING PICTURE PUZZLES—SIMPLE

Up and down, round and round

Kemah, Texas, initially was a small fishing village, but today it is a popular family vacation destination.

SIMPLE

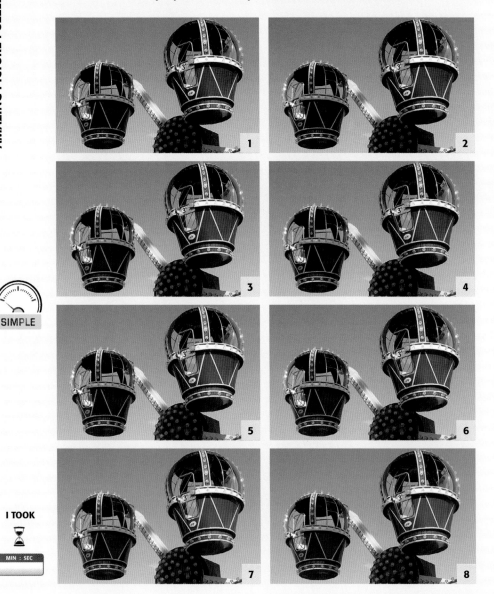

I TOOK

MIN : SEC

SOLUTION ON PAGE 259

Blossoms so pretty

Geisha culture emerged in the eighteenth century. Traditionally, geishas are entertainers who sing, dance, and recite poetry.

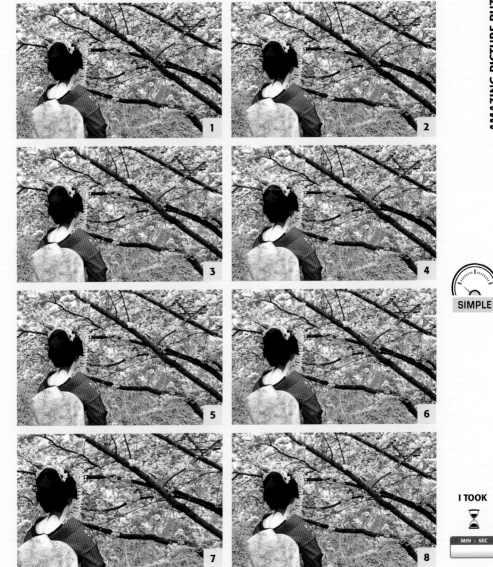

SIMPLE

I TOOK

MIN : SEC

SOLUTION ON PAGE 260

My first tricycle

Before this little pup progresses to a bicycle, try and spot all the differences between these two images.

DID YOU KNOW?
Pugs originate from China. They were popularized in western Europe by the House of Orange of the Netherlands.

SIMPLE

I TOOK

MIN : SEC

THE DIFFERENCES I SPOTTED

09 ○○○○○○○○○

SOLUTION ON PAGE 260

Spool me silly

"There is no time for cut-and-dried monotony. There is time for work. And time for love. That leaves no other time."
— Coco Chanel

DID YOU KNOW?
*The perfume Chanel No. 5 was the first to be a blend
of a variety of floral scents.*

DIFFICULT

I TOOK

MIN : SEC

THE DIFFERENCES I SPOTTED

10 ○○○○○○○○○○

SOLUTION ON PAGE 262

When in Rome...

It is very common practice in Italian villages and towns for the townspeople to celebrate festivities by cooking and eating together.

DIFFICULT

I TOOK

MIN : SEC

SOLUTION ON PAGE 262

Whatever you do, don't look down!

The world's first Ferris wheel was erected in 1893, by George Washington Gale Ferris Jr. at the World's Columbian Exposition in Chicago.

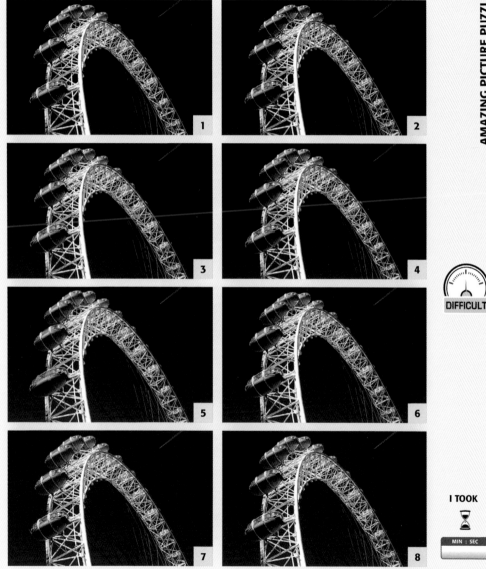

DIFFICULT

I TOOK

MIN : SEC

SOLUTION ON PAGE 262

A feathery bunch

Try and find all the differences between these images and beat the clock.

DIFFICULT

I TOOK

MIN : SEC

THE DIFFERENCES I SPOTTED

07 ○○○○○○○

SOLUTION ON PAGE 262

Round table conference

The meeting is in session. Before it concludes, spot all the differences between the images.

DIFFICULT

I TOOK

MIN : SEC

THE DIFFERENCES I SPOTTED

08 ○○○○○○○○

SOLUTION ON PAGE 262

I'm always ready for Mardi Gras

The Venetian mask that covers the entire face was traditionally worn as a piece of art and is called the *bauta*.

DIFFICULT

I TOOK

MIN : SEC

THE DIFFERENCES I SPOTTED

08 ○○○○○○○○

SOLUTION ON PAGE 262

Building a better tomorrow

Architects have eyes for detail. Can you spot the differences between the two images?

DIFFICULT

I TOOK

MIN : SEC

THE DIFFERENCES I SPOTTED

06 ○○○○○○

SOLUTION ON PAGE 263

Olympic Port in Barcelona

The Olympic Port in Barcelona was made in honor of the
1992 Olympic Games by Frank Gehry.

DIFFICULT

I TOOK

MIN : SEC

THE DIFFERENCES I SPOTTED

08 ○○○○○○○○

SOLUTION ON PAGE 263

Crimson all around me

Beacon Hill in Boston is known to have been home to many notable residents, like Sylvia Plath, Robert Frost, and Uma Thurman.

DIFFICULT

I TOOK

MIN : SEC

THE DIFFERENCES I SPOTTED

07 ○○○○○○○

SOLUTION ON PAGE 263

Giddy up!

The concept of "cowboys" originated in Spain. They brought this method of cattle ranching to America in the sixteenth century.

DIFFICULT

I TOOK

MIN : SEC

THE DIFFERENCES I SPOTTED

SOLUTION ON PAGE 263

Summer fun

Tulum, Playa del Carmen, Huatulco, and Acapulco are some of the top beaches of Mexico.

DIFFICULT

I TOOK

MIN : SEC

THE DIFFERENCES I SPOTTED

06 ○○○○○○

SOLUTION ON PAGE 263

Laughter among friends

Can you see all the differences between the two images?

DIFFICULT

I TOOK

MIN : SEC

THE DIFFERENCES I SPOTTED

08

SOLUTION ON PAGE 263

Now, let's go there

While these hikers decide which mountain to conquer next,
see if you can find all the differences between the two images.

DIFFICULT

I TOOK

MIN : SEC

THE DIFFERENCES I SPOTTED

SOLUTION ON PAGE 264

The love boat

The Gondoliers, set in Venice, is a two-act comic operetta written by Gilbert and Sullivan.

DIFFICULT

I TOOK

MIN : SEC

THE DIFFERENCES I SPOTTED

07 ○○○○○○○

SOLUTION ON PAGE 264

Not your budget hotel
The Luxor Hotel and Casino's entire decor is inspired by ancient Egypt.

DIFFICULT

I TOOK

MIN : SEC

THE DIFFERENCES I SPOTTED
05 ○○○○○

SOLUTION ON PAGE 264

A yellow horse!

Sea horses don't have scales; they have bony plates under their skin that serves and looks like armor.

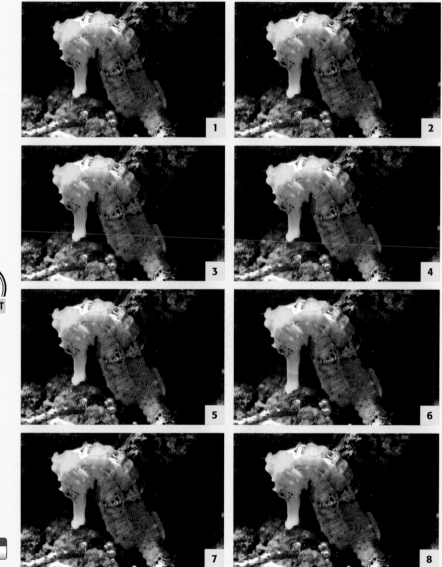

DIFFICULT

I TOOK

MIN : SEC

SOLUTION ON PAGE 264

Cock-a-doodle-doo

From this lot, there is an odd rooster. Can you find him, as he is urgently needed to wake up the other animals?

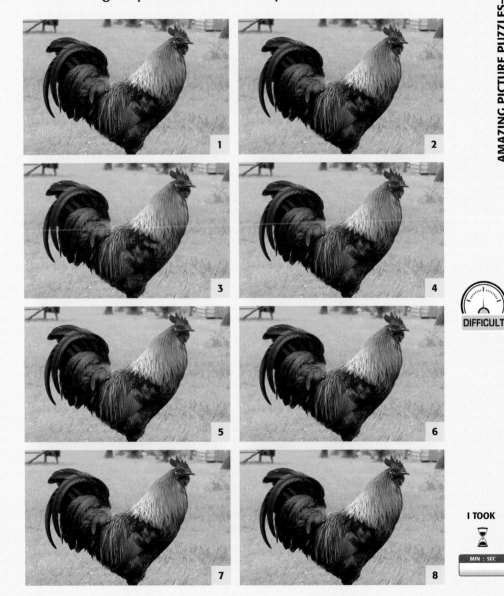

DIFFICULT

I TOOK

MIN : SEC

SOLUTION ON PAGE 264

Tranquility personified

With a calm mind, try and spot all the differences between these two beautiful images.

DID YOU KNOW?
The Mughal emperor Aurangzeb destroyed the original Golden Temple and built a mosque in its place.

DIFFICULT

I TOOK

MIN : SEC

THE DIFFERENCES I SPOTTED

 ○○○○○○○○○○

SOLUTION ON PAGE 264

The most crooked

Lombard Street in San Francisco is the most crooked street in the world.

DIFFICULT

I TOOK

MIN : SEC

THE DIFFERENCES I SPOTTED

07

SOLUTION ON PAGE 265

Days of glory past

The Parthenon was a temple dedicated to the Greek goddess Athena, whom the people of Athens considered their protector.

DIFFICULT

I TOOK

MIN : SEC

THE DIFFERENCES I SPOTTED

08 ○○○○○○○○

SOLUTION ON PAGE 265

Flipper's day out

A bottlenose dolphin can live up to fifty years.

DIFFICULT

I TOOK

MIN : SEC

THE DIFFERENCES I SPOTTED

06 ○○○○○○

SOLUTION ON PAGE 265

You get all kinds

"A mere friend will agree with you but a real friend will argue."
— Russian proverb

DIFFICULT

I TOOK

MIN : SEC

THE DIFFERENCES I SPOTTED

06 ○○○○○○

SOLUTION ON PAGE 265

Office space

Spot all the differences between the images.

DIFFICULT

I TOOK

MIN : SEC

THE DIFFERENCES I SPOTTED

09 ○○○○○○○○○

SOLUTION ON PAGE 265

A picnic for you and me

While the children are still busy, try and see if you can find all the differences between these two images.

DIFFICULT

I TOOK

MIN : SEC

THE DIFFERENCES I SPOTTED

07 ○○○○○○○

SOLUTION ON PAGE 265

The Windy City

Chicago is the largest city in Illinois. It is also the third-most populated city in the United States.

DIFFICULT

I TOOK

MIN : SEC

THE DIFFERENCES I SPOTTED

08 ○○○○○○○○

SOLUTION ON PAGE 266

A Boston view

Boston is the capital and the largest city of the state of Massachusetts.

DIFFICULT

I TOOK

MIN : SEC

THE DIFFERENCES I SPOTTED

SOLUTION ON PAGE 266

Bear hug!

"You can't wrap love in a box, but you can wrap a person in a hug." — Unknown

DIFFICULT

I TOOK

MIN : SEC

THE DIFFERENCES I SPOTTED

06

SOLUTION ON PAGE 266

Nature never ceases to amaze

Try and spot all the differences between these images as quickly as you can.

DIFFICULT

I TOOK

MIN : SEC

THE DIFFERENCES I SPOTTED

07 ○○○○○○○

SOLUTION ON PAGE 266

Her special day

Everything is perfect, except one image. Can you find it?

DIFFICULT

I TOOK

MIN : SEC

SOLUTION ON PAGE 266

Punch!
Don't break into a sweat. Try and find the odd one out.

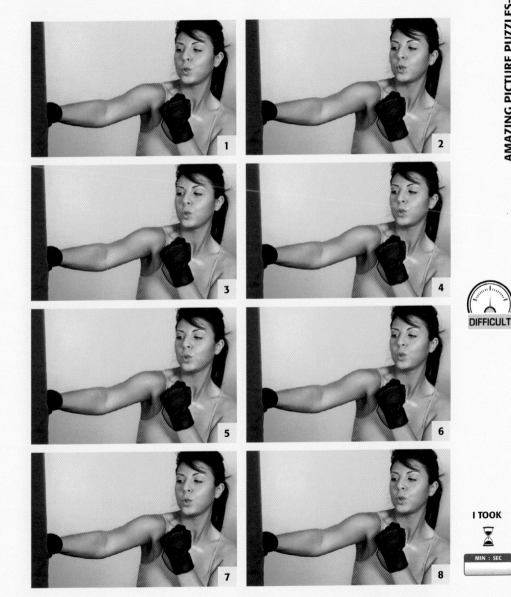

DIFFICULT

I TOOK

MIN : SEC

SOLUTION ON PAGE 266

Round and round we go

"I see nothing in space as promising as the view from a Ferris wheel." — E. B. White

DID YOU KNOW?
Navy Pier is on the shoreline of Lake Michigan in Chicago. It was built in 1916 by Daniel Burnham.

DIFFICULT

I TOOK

MIN : SEC

THE DIFFERENCES I SPOTTED

08

○○○○○○○○

SOLUTION ON PAGE 267

Look at me
"It is not only fine feathers that make fine birds." — Aesop

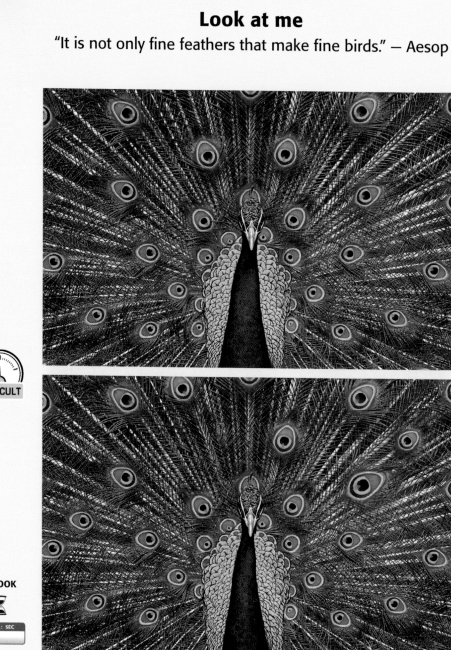

DIFFICULT

I TOOK

MIN : SEC

THE DIFFERENCES I SPOTTED

06 ○○○○○○

SOLUTION ON PAGE 267

You looking at me?

The kudu antelope's horn is used as a musical instrument in many cultures. It is often used in Jewish ceremonies and is called a *shofar*.

DIFFICULT

I TOOK

MIN : SEC

THE DIFFERENCES I SPOTTED

07 ○○○○○○○

SOLUTION ON PAGE 267

And the calorie count is on!

As they try and meet their target, see if you can spot all the differences between these images.

DIFFICULT

I TOOK

MIN : SEC

THE DIFFERENCES I SPOTTED

09 ○○○○○○○○○

SOLUTION ON PAGE 267

Celebrating the free spirit

"The Divine Spirit does not reside in any, except the joyful heart."
— The Talmud

DIFFICULT

I TOOK

MIN : SEC

THE DIFFERENCES I SPOTTED

07 ⟩ ○○○○○○○

SOLUTION ON PAGE 267

Color in every step I take

"A rose must remain with the sun, but with the rain its lovely promise won't come true." — Ray Evans

DIFFICULT

I TOOK

MIN : SEC

SOLUTION ON PAGE 267

The zebra of the city

As quickly as you can, spot the odd image.

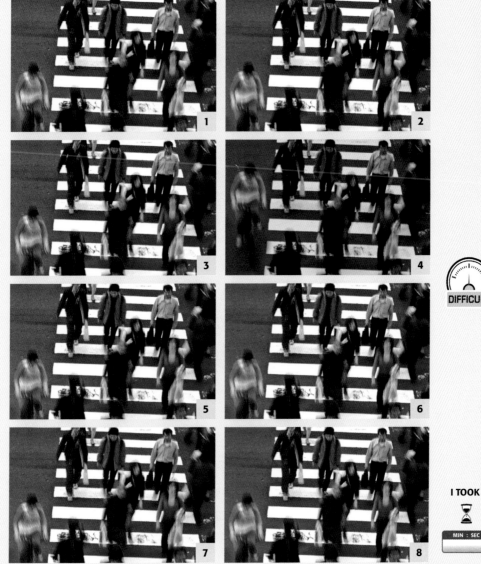

DIFFICULT

I TOOK

MIN : SEC

SOLUTION ON PAGE 268

Success is a state of mind

With friends like this, anything is possible. Invite a friend to join you as you solve this puzzle to make it more enjoyable.

DIFFICULT

I TOOK

MIN : SEC

THE DIFFERENCES I SPOTTED

07 ○○○○○○○

SOLUTION ON PAGE 268

Cute and grumpy

Koalas are found on the coastal region of Australia, between Adelaide and Cape York Peninsula.

DIFFICULT

I TOOK

MIN : SEC

THE DIFFERENCES I SPOTTED

06 ○○○○○○

SOLUTION ON PAGE 268

Universally treasured

"Grandma always made you feel she had been waiting to see just you all day and now the day was complete." – Marcy DeMaree

DIFFICULT

I TOOK

MIN : SEC

THE DIFFERENCES I SPOTTED

07 ○○○○○○○

SOLUTION ON PAGE 268

Connected by smiles

Smiling is a natural way to express pleasure, and make one more likable and approachable.

DIFFICULT

I TOOK

MIN : SEC

THE DIFFERENCES I SPOTTED
06 ○○○○○○

SOLUTION ON PAGE 268

Hello, Seattle!

All these images seem alike, but one of them is different.
Can you spot it?

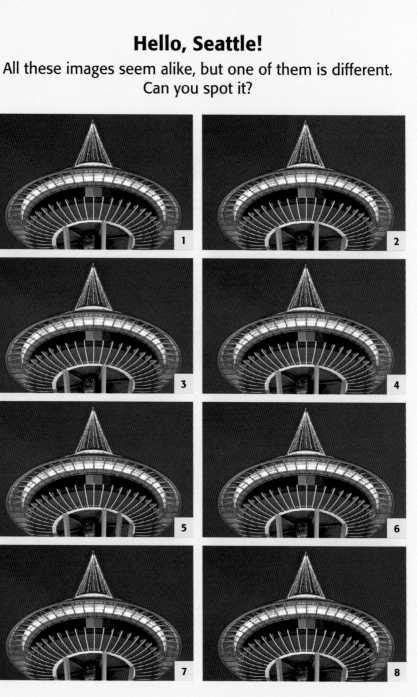

DIFFICULT

I TOOK

MIN : SEC

SOLUTION ON PAGE 268

Tap away to Chicago

The musical *Chicago* is set during the time of Prohibition. It is based on actual criminals and crimes reported by Maurine Dallas Watkins.

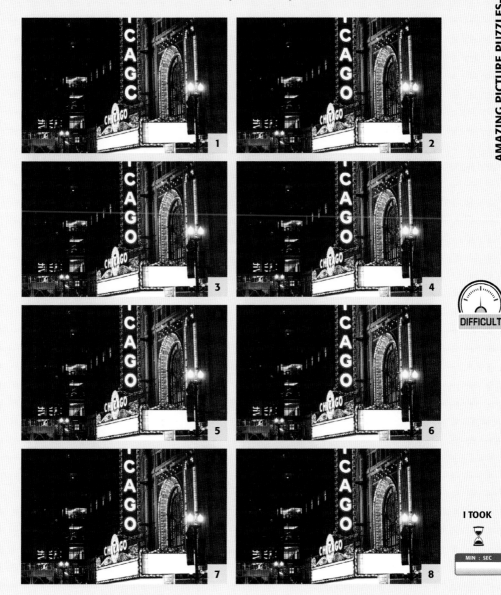

DIFFICULT

I TOOK

MIN : SEC

SOLUTION ON PAGE 269

Three stooges

"Love will draw an elephant through a key-hole."
— Samuel Richardson

DIFFICULT

I TOOK

MIN : SEC

THE DIFFERENCES I SPOTTED

SOLUTION ON PAGE 269

I need to test the water first

In ancient times, the giraffe was associated with the *qilin*, a mythical Chinese creature.

DIFFICULT

I TOOK

MIN : SEC

THE DIFFERENCES I SPOTTED

06 ○○○○○○

SOLUTION ON PAGE 269

Friendly huddle!

Before this fun group disperses, try and locate all the differences between the images.

DIFFICULT

I TOOK

MIN : SEC

THE DIFFERENCES I SPOTTED

SOLUTION ON PAGE 269

The pillars of our world

"The mark of a true professional is giving more than you get."
— Unknown

DIFFICULT

I TOOK

MIN : SEC

THE DIFFERENCES I SPOTTED

09 ○○○○○○○○○

SOLUTION ON PAGE 269

Bike city

Before the owner finds his bicycle, try and spot all the differences between these two images.

DIFFICULT

I TOOK

MIN : SEC

THE DIFFERENCES I SPOTTED

SOLUTION ON PAGE 269

A beauty of tradition
Traditional Chinese multistory buildings are called *lou*.

DIFFICULT

I TOOK

MIN : SEC

THE DIFFERENCES I SPOTTED

08 ○○○○○○

SOLUTION ON PAGE 270

AMAZING PICTURE PUZZLES—DIFFICULT

Underwater tigers

These images might look similar, but there are seven differences. Try and spot them.

DIFFICULT

I TOOK

MIN : SEC

THE DIFFERENCES I SPOTTED

07 ○○○○○○○

SOLUTION ON PAGE 270

Nuts!

Squirrels are omnivores and are found in
Asia, Europe, Africa, and the Americas.

DIFFICULT

I TOOK

MIN : SEC

THE DIFFERENCES I SPOTTED

05

○○○○○

SOLUTION ON PAGE 270

Boom! Boom! Boom!

In 1641, the modern Brazilian Carnival originated in
Rio de Janeiro.

DIFFICULT

I TOOK

MIN : SEC

THE DIFFERENCES I SPOTTED

06 ○○○○○○

SOLUTION ON PAGE 270

Friendly faces

See if you can work out where all the differences between these two images are.

DIFFICULT

I TOOK

MIN : SEC

THE DIFFERENCES I SPOTTED

08 ○○○○○○○○○

SOLUTION ON PAGE 270

Market of color

Try and spot all the differences between these colorful images.

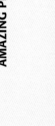

DIFFICULT

I TOOK

MIN : SEC

THE DIFFERENCES I SPOTTED

SOLUTION ON PAGE 270

Colorful Singapore!

Singapore is located in Southeast Asia, and is one of the most densely populated countries in the world.

DIFFICULT

I TOOK

MIN : SEC

THE DIFFERENCES I SPOTTED

08 ○○○○○○○○

SOLUTION ON PAGE 271

I've got my eye on you

Found on the eastern side of South Africa, the eastern green mamba is the smallest member of the mamba family.

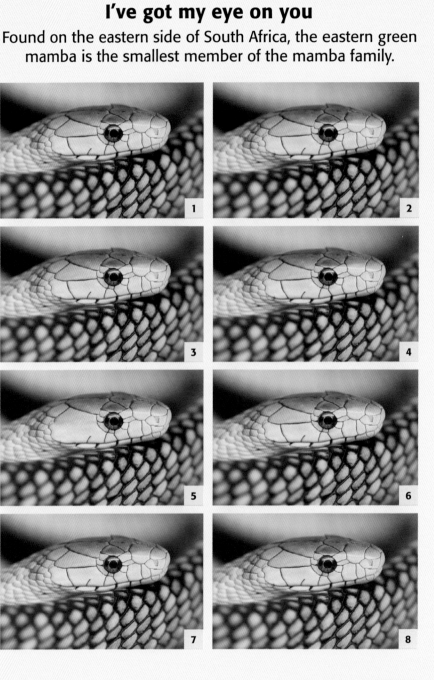

DIFFICULT

I TOOK

MIN : SEC

SOLUTION ON PAGE 271

Gliding along

Solve this puzzle as quickly as you can and cruise to the next level, just like this little slug.

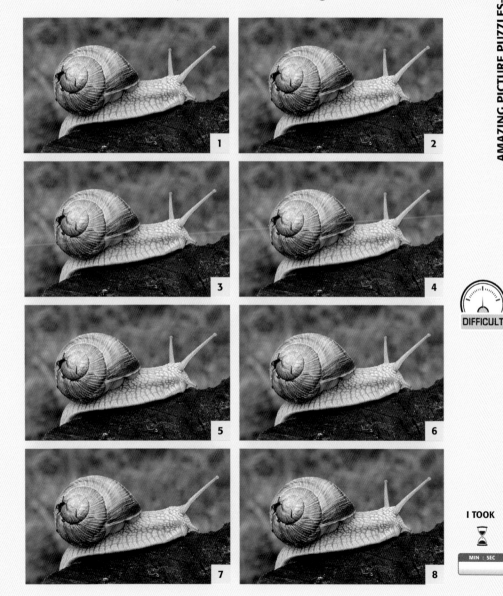

DIFFICULT

I TOOK

MIN : SEC

SOLUTION ON PAGE 271

Drum roll, please!

As the band cheers you on, try and spot all the differences between the two images.

DID YOU KNOW?
Bands of America organizes marching band competitions between high schools across the United States, the biggest being the Grand National Championships.

DIFFICULT

I TOOK

MIN : SEC

THE DIFFERENCES I SPOTTED

08 ○○○○○○○○

SOLUTION ON PAGE 271

Sunny banana

Many Thai cities are famous for their floating markets, which are basically boats selling fruits and vegetables.

DIFFICULT

I TOOK

MIN : SEC

THE DIFFERENCES I SPOTTED

SOLUTION ON PAGE 271

Bling!

Dubai is a place famous for its tax-free luxury goods,
which include gold jewelry.

DIFFICULT

I TOOK

MIN : SEC

THE DIFFERENCES I SPOTTED

08 ○○○○○○○○

SOLUTION ON PAGE 271

We share everything

Before this group of friends finishes their drink,
try and find all the differences between the images.

DIFFICULT

I TOOK

MIN : SEC

THE DIFFERENCES I SPOTTED

07 ○○○○○○○

SOLUTION ON PAGE 272

A family outing

The African elephant can easily be distinguished from the Indian elephant, as it is much larger in size and its ears are also bigger.

DIFFICULT

I TOOK

MIN : SEC

THE DIFFERENCES I SPOTTED

08 ○○○○○○○○

SOLUTION ON PAGE 272

Girls just wanna have fun!

Get into the groove and try to spot all the differences between the two images.

DIFFICULT

I TOOK

MIN : SEC

THE DIFFERENCES I SPOTTED

06 ○○○○○○

SOLUTION ON PAGE 272

Scuba duba doo!

A natural inspiration, the Great Barrier Reef is one of the Seven Wonders of the World.

DIFFICULT

I TOOK

MIN : SEC

THE DIFFERENCES I SPOTTED

07 ○○○○○○○

SOLUTION ON PAGE 272

Sundown at the dock

In addition to its nightlife, Barcelona is also very popular for yachting.

DIFFICULT

I TOOK

MIN : SEC

THE DIFFERENCES I SPOTTED

07 ○○○○○○○

SOLUTION ON PAGE 272

Local shopping

If pyramids and budget shopping interest you,
Cairo is the place to go.

DIFFICULT

I TOOK

MIN : SEC

THE DIFFERENCES I SPOTTED

08 ○○○○○○○○○

SOLUTION ON PAGE 272

Honeylicious

Throughout history, honeybee communities have been used in literature to symbolize human society.

DIFFICULT

I TOOK

MIN : SEC

THE DIFFERENCES I SPOTTED

07 ○○○○○○○

SOLUTION ON PAGE 273

Who you calling a guinea pig?

Guinea pigs are commonly called cavies, as they belong to the Cavidae rodent family.

DIFFICULT

I TOOK

MIN : SEC

THE DIFFERENCES I SPOTTED

05 ○○○○○

SOLUTION ON PAGE 273

Splendor in the grass

The grand Caucasus mountain range is located in four
countries: Armenia, Azerbaijan, Georgia, and Russia.

DIFFICULT

I TOOK

MIN : SEC

THE DIFFERENCES I SPOTTED

08 ○○○○○○○○

SOLUTION ON PAGE 273

Sunny family portrait

Sit down, relax, and see if you can spot all the differences between these two images.

DIFFICULT

I TOOK

MIN : SEC

THE DIFFERENCES I SPOTTED

08 ○○○○○○○○○

SOLUTION ON PAGE 273

Canal city of romance

"Love is three quarters curiosity." — Giacomo Casanova

DIFFICULT

I TOOK

MIN : SEC

THE DIFFERENCES I SPOTTED

SOLUTION ON PAGE 273

A romantic Grecian night

"Love is composed of a single soul inhabiting two bodies."
— Aristotle

DIFFICULT

I TOOK

MIN : SEC

THE DIFFERENCES I SPOTTED

09 ○○○○○○○○○

SOLUTION ON PAGE 273

Man's best friend

Heterochromia, which is the condition of having different colored eyes, is common among huskies.

DIFFICULT

I TOOK

MIN : SEC

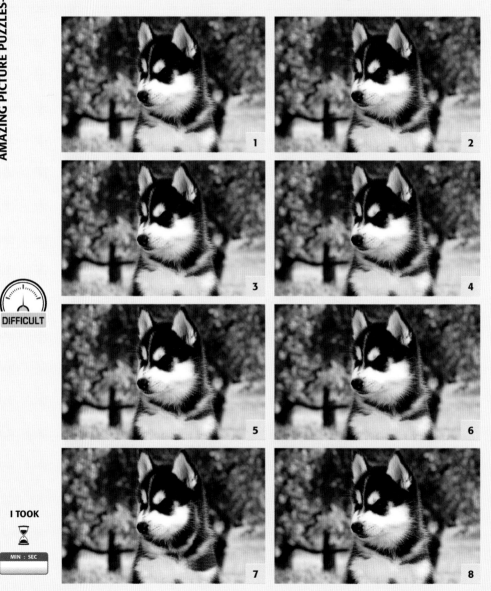

SOLUTION ON PAGE 274

Yes, we look a lot alike

Colobus monkeys are born completely white and will gain their black-and-white coloring at around three months old.

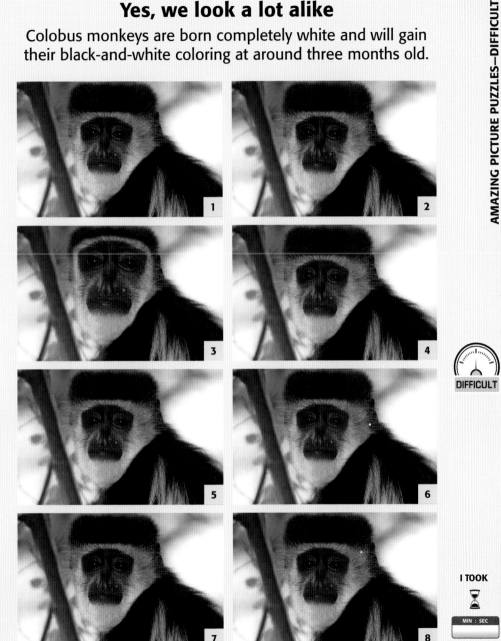

DIFFICULT

I TOOK

MIN : SEC

SOLUTION ON PAGE 274

Another pilgrimage
Pray tell me, can you spot the odd one out?

DIFFICULT

I TOOK

MIN : SEC

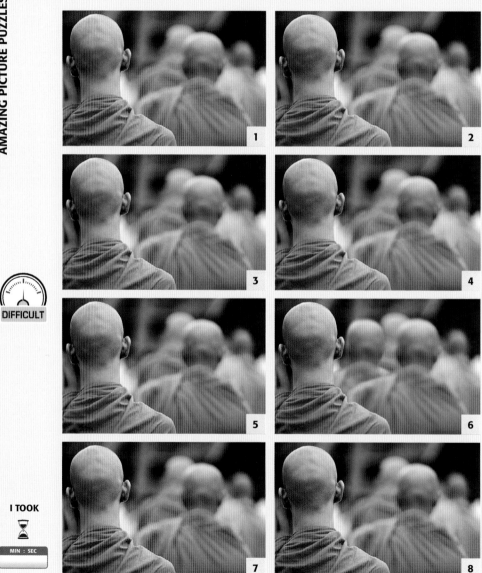

SOLUTION ON PAGE 274

Let's go fly a kite, up to the highest height!

Julie Andrews won an Oscar, a Golden Globe, and a British Academy Award for her role in *Mary Poppins* (1964).

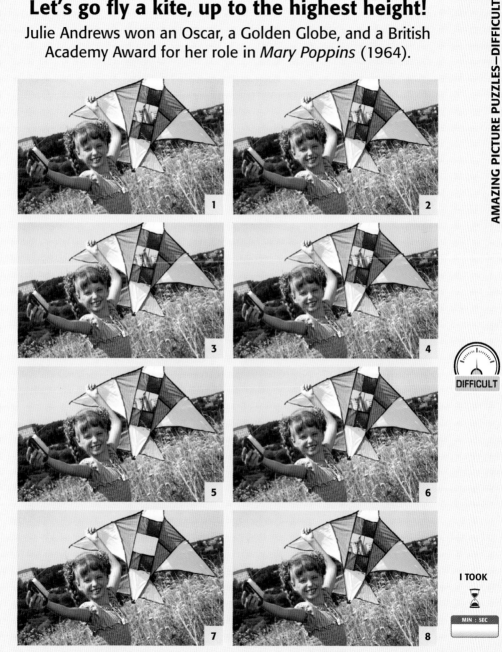

DIFFICULT

I TOOK

MIN : SEC

SOLUTION ON PAGE 274

Colorful culture

Caminito is a street in Buenos Aires, the capital of Argentina.

DID YOU KNOW?

Most of Buenos Aires is highly influenced by Italian culture and traditions, due to its early settlers being from European nations.

DIFFICULT

I TOOK

MIN : SEC

THE DIFFERENCES I SPOTTED

08 ○○○○○○○○

SOLUTION ON PAGE 274

Fish sprinkles

Solving this puzzle may seem very complicated, but it's really as fun as swimming through a coral reef.

DID YOU KNOW?
Coral reefs form some of the most diverse ecosystems of the planet and are therefore referred to as the rain forests of the sea.

COMPLEX

I TOOK

MIN : SEC

THE DIFFERENCES I SPOTTED

10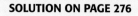

SOLUTION ON PAGE 276

Step up! Shape up!

Give your mind a mental workout by locating the odd one out.

COMPLEX

I TOOK

MIN : SEC

SOLUTION ON PAGE 276

The loser pays for lunch

Before the race concludes, can you spot the odd one out?

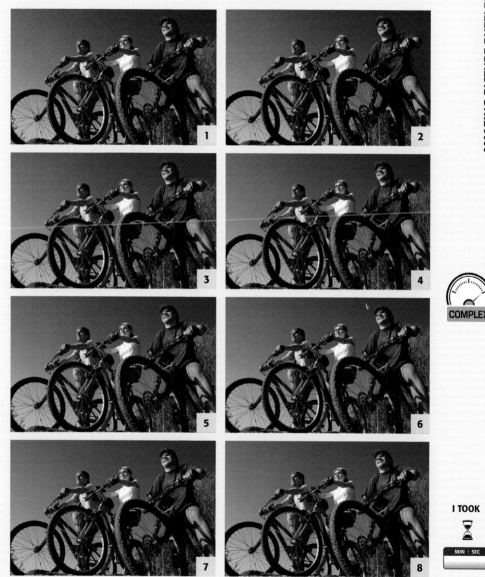

COMPLEX

I TOOK

MIN : SEC

SOLUTION ON PAGE 276

Only food on my mind

Madrid is widely known for its nightlife and soccer but the true essence of the Spanish capital lies in the food.

COMPLEX

I TOOK

MIN : SEC

THE DIFFERENCES I SPOTTED

08 ○○○○○○○○

SOLUTION ON PAGE 276

Street of light

Celebrated on the 15th day of the Spring Festival is the Shanghai Lantern Festival at Yuyuan Garden, also known as Shanghai Old Street.

COMPLEX

I TOOK

MIN : SEC

THE DIFFERENCES I SPOTTED

06 ○○○○○○

SOLUTION ON PAGE 276

The grass is greener

Optimism makes for a great companion. Don't give up until you find all the differences between these two images.

COMPLEX

I TOOK

MIN : SEC

THE DIFFERENCES I SPOTTED

08 ○○○○○○○○

SOLUTION ON PAGE 276

Teamwork pays

Make this puzzle even more fun by asking a friend
to help you solve it!

COMPLEX

I TOOK

MIN : SEC

THE DIFFERENCES I SPOTTED

06 ○○○○○○

SOLUTION ON PAGE 277

Huddle up!

Walter Camp, popularly known as the "Father of American Football," formed the rules of the sport.

COMPLEX

I TOOK

MIN : SEC

THE DIFFERENCES I SPOTTED

07 ⊙⊙⊙⊙⊙⊙⊙

SOLUTION ON PAGE 277

Racing for health

Time is racing by! See how quickly you can find all the differences between the two images.

COMPLEX

I TOOK

MIN : SEC

THE DIFFERENCES I SPOTTED

05 ○○○○○

SOLUTION ON PAGE 277

Party town!

Las Vegas is known for its over-the-top parties that practically take place on streets.

COMPLEX

I TOOK

MIN : SEC

THE DIFFERENCES I SPOTTED

06 ○○○○○○

SOLUTION ON PAGE 277

The train leaves in ten minutes

Before the train leaves Grand Central Station, try and spot all the differences between the two images.

COMPLEX

I TOOK

MIN : SEC

THE DIFFERENCES I SPOTTED

08 ○○○○○○○○

SOLUTION ON PAGE 277

Berry blast!

Quick! Before this little one finishes his snack,
try and solve this puzzle.

COMPLEX

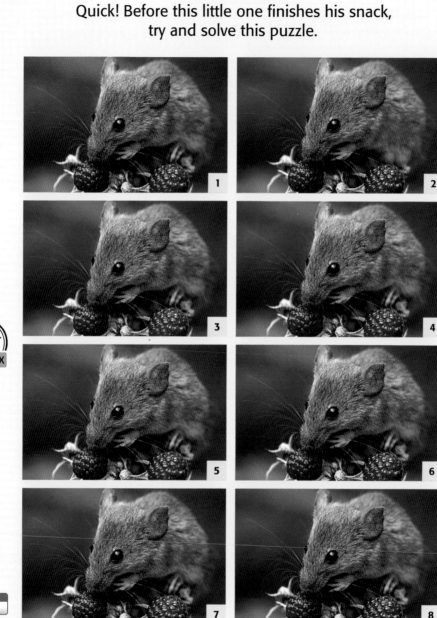

I TOOK

MIN : SEC

SOLUTION ON PAGE 277

Snowy halo

The *Goura victoria* is also known as the Victoria crowned pigeon, in honor of the British Queen Victoria.

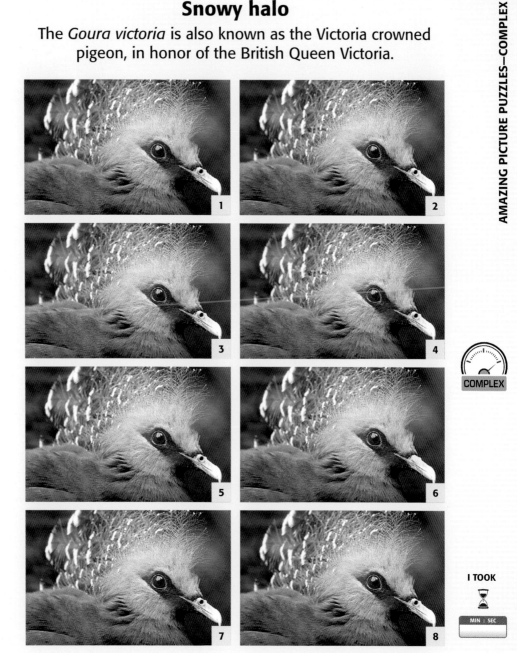

COMPLEX

I TOOK

MIN : SEC

SOLUTION ON PAGE 278

Let's celebrate!

As this happy family celebrates the joys of life, try and spot the differences between these two images.

COMPLEX

I TOOK

MIN : SEC

THE DIFFERENCES I SPOTTED

09 ○○○○○○○○○

SOLUTION ON PAGE 278

Mapping the future

"An economist is an expert who will know tomorrow why the things he predicted yesterday didn't happen today." — Laurence J. Peter

COMPLEX

I TOOK

MIN : SEC

THE DIFFERENCES I SPOTTED

08 ○○○○○○○○

SOLUTION ON PAGE 278

AMAZING PICTURE PUZZLES–COMPLEX

Bumper to bumper

The traffic in all the images looks the same, but that is not so. Can you spot the one that is different?

COMPLEX

I TOOK

MIN : SEC

SOLUTION ON PAGE 278

Sunny San Francisco!

All the pictures of this bus may look the same, but that is not the case. Can you tell which is the odd one out?

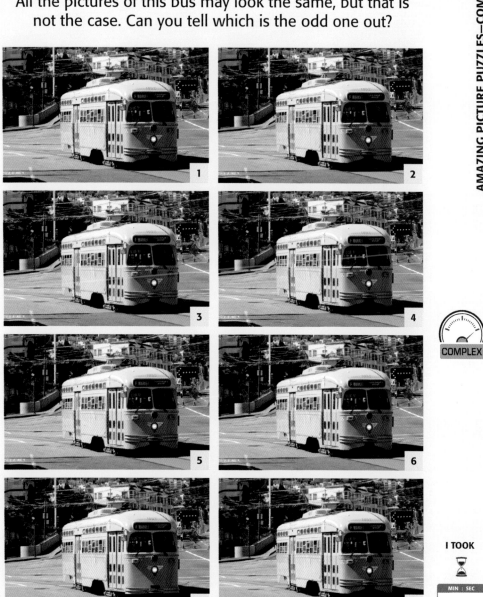

COMPLEX

I TOOK

MIN : SEC

SOLUTION ON PAGE 278

Bee silly!

Shredded bee larvae served with rice is a popular Indonesian delicacy.

I TOOK

MIN : SEC

THE DIFFERENCES I SPOTTED

08

SOLUTION ON PAGE 278

Lunch time!

Try and find all the differences between these two adorable images.

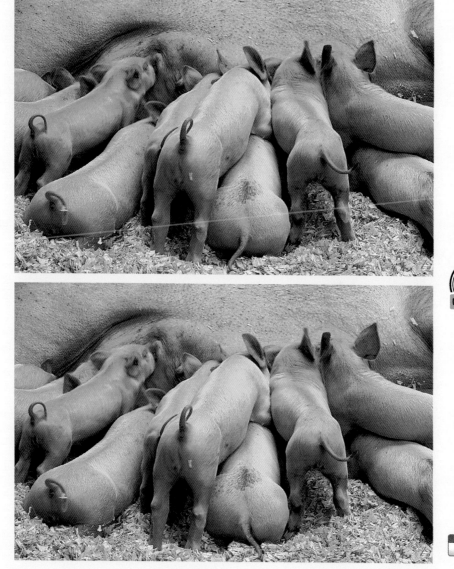

COMPLEX

I TOOK

MIN : SEC

THE DIFFERENCES I SPOTTED

08 ○○○○○○○○○

SOLUTION ON PAGE 279

We'll shop but never drop

These girls are on the quest to find the perfect dress.
Can you find the differences between the two images?

COMPLEX

I TOOK

MIN : SEC

THE DIFFERENCES I SPOTTED

06 ○○○○○○

SOLUTION ON PAGE 279

Nothing less than perfection will do

Work up an appetite by attempting to find all the differences between the two images.

COMPLEX

I TOOK

MIN : SEC

THE DIFFERENCES I SPOTTED

10 ○○○○○○○○○○

SOLUTION ON PAGE 279

A romantic dinner just for you

Over time, Venice has earned itself many nicknames. "City of Masks," "The Floating City," and "City of Canals" are just a few.

DID YOU KNOW?
Venice is pronounced as Venezia in Italian and it is the capital of the region Veneto.

COMPLEX

I TOOK

MIN : SEC

THE DIFFERENCES I SPOTTED

SOLUTION ON PAGE 279

My little ballerina

While all these pups look as cute as one another, one of them stands out more than the rest. Can you spot it?

COMPLEX

I TOOK

MIN : SEC

SOLUTION ON PAGE 279

Friends forever

"A real friend is one who walks in when the rest of the world walks out." — Walter Winchell

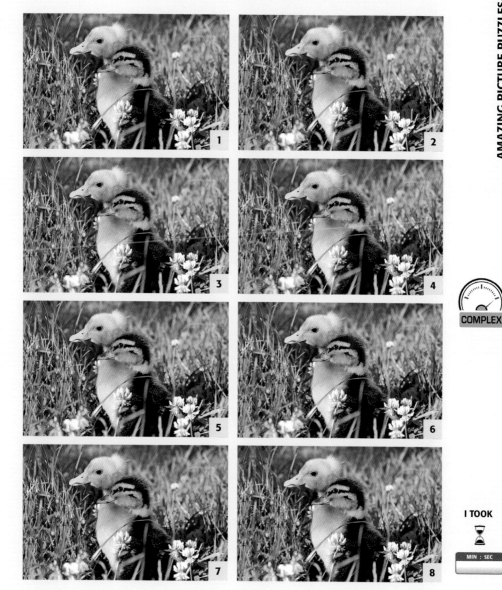

COMPLEX

I TOOK

MIN : SEC

SOLUTION ON PAGE 279

Live for today, plan for tomorrow, party tonight!

Before you go partying all night, try and find the differences between the two images.

COMPLEX

I TOOK

MIN : SEC

THE DIFFERENCES I SPOTTED

SOLUTION ON PAGE 280

The game just got even more interesting

See how well you score against the clock. Try and find all the differences between the two images as quickly as possible.

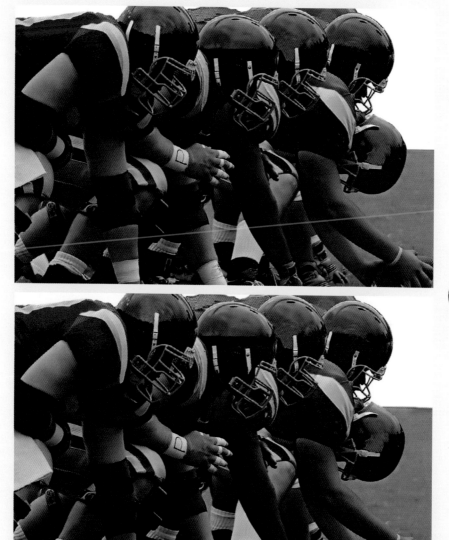

COMPLEX

I TOOK

MIN : SEC

THE DIFFERENCES I SPOTTED

06 ○○○○○○

SOLUTION ON PAGE 280

Bike or train?

While you're contemplating that thought, try and spot all the differences between these two images.

COMPLEX

I TOOK

MIN : SEC

THE DIFFERENCES I SPOTTED

08 ○○○○○○○○

SOLUTION ON PAGE 280

Shop till you drop

"I always say shopping is cheaper than a psychiatrist."
— Tammy Faye Bakker

COMPLEX

I TOOK

MIN : SEC

THE DIFFERENCES I SPOTTED

07 ○○○○○○○

SOLUTION ON PAGE 280

Only fodder on my mind

You can tell the age of a cow by counting the number of rings on its horn.

COMPLEX

I TOOK

MIN : SEC

THE DIFFERENCES I SPOTTED

08 ○○○○○○○○

SOLUTION ON PAGE 280

The result of nature's creative moods

Even though these images look alike, there are a few differences.

COMPLEX

I TOOK

MIN : SEC

THE DIFFERENCES I SPOTTED

SOLUTION ON PAGE 280

Save the last dance for me

Before the sun sets, spot the odd image.

COMPLEX

I TOOK

MIN : SEC

SOLUTION ON PAGE 281

Say cheese!

Picture perfect, but one. Can you locate it?

COMPLEX

I TOOK

MIN : SEC

SOLUTION ON PAGE 281

The bustle at the square

Before these people disperse, see if you can spot all the differences between these two images.

DID YOU KNOW?
Moscow, the capital of Russia, is the most populous city in Europe.

COMPLEX

I TOOK

MIN : SEC

THE DIFFERENCES I SPOTTED

09 ○○○○○○○○○

SOLUTION ON PAGE 281

Waddle this way

Before this waddling bunch heads home, try and find all the differences between the two images.

COMPLEX

I TOOK

MIN : SEC

THE DIFFERENCES I SPOTTED

09 ○○○○○○○○○

SOLUTION ON PAGE 281

I'm swimming right at you
Before this fish nips you, quickly solve the puzzle.

COMPLEX

I TOOK

MIN : SEC

THE DIFFERENCES I SPOTTED

07 ○○○○○○○

SOLUTION ON PAGE 281

AMAZING PICTURE PUZZLES—COMPLEX

Blurry

We know it's getting harder to see, but give it your best shot and find all the differences between the two images.

COMPLEX

I TOOK

MIN : SEC

THE DIFFERENCES I SPOTTED

07 ○○○○○○○

SOLUTION ON PAGE 281

Happy birthday!

Even if it's not your birthday today, have some fun by finding the differences between these images.

COMPLEX

I TOOK

MIN : SEC

THE DIFFERENCES I SPOTTED

08 ○○○○○○○○

SOLUTION ON PAGE 282

AMAZING PICTURE PUZZLES—COMPLEX

My very own houseboat

Spot all the differences between these two images.

COMPLEX

I TOOK

MIN : SEC

THE DIFFERENCES I SPOTTED

07 ○○○○○○○

SOLUTION ON PAGE 282

Sunset at the pier

The day has come to an end, but the fun doesn't have to stop. Solve this puzzle with a friend and keep the fun alive!

COMPLEX

I TOOK

MIN : SEC

THE DIFFERENCES I SPOTTED

05 ○○○○○

SOLUTION ON PAGE 282

Parrot talk

Before this pretty lot flies home, find all the differences between the images.

COMPLEX

I TOOK

MIN : SEC

THE DIFFERENCES I SPOTTED

09 ○○○○○○○○○

SOLUTION ON PAGE 282

Who are you calling a chicken?

Without getting your feathers ruffled, try and find all the differences between these two images.

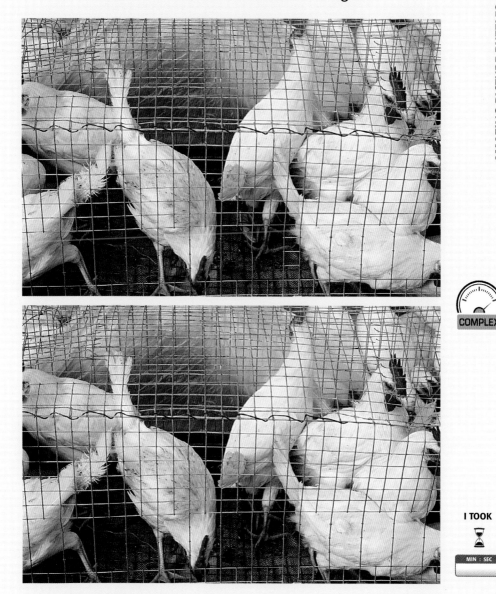

COMPLEX

I TOOK

MIN : SEC

THE DIFFERENCES I SPOTTED

07 ⊕ ○○○○○○○○

SOLUTION ON PAGE 282

Santa Claus is coming to town

A mixture of secular and religious traditions, Christmas is a holiday celebrated by people from all around the world.

COMPLEX

I TOOK

MIN : SEC

THE DIFFERENCES I SPOTTED

07

SOLUTION ON PAGE 282

And a one, two, three

As they complete their workout, see if you can work out where all the differences between these two images are.

COMPLEX

I TOOK

MIN : SEC

THE DIFFERENCES I SPOTTED

05 ○○○○○

SOLUTION ON PAGE 283

Now that's a lot of laundry!

Dhobi Ghat, the washer's area in Mumbai, is a system where the laundry of the residents can all be done at one time.

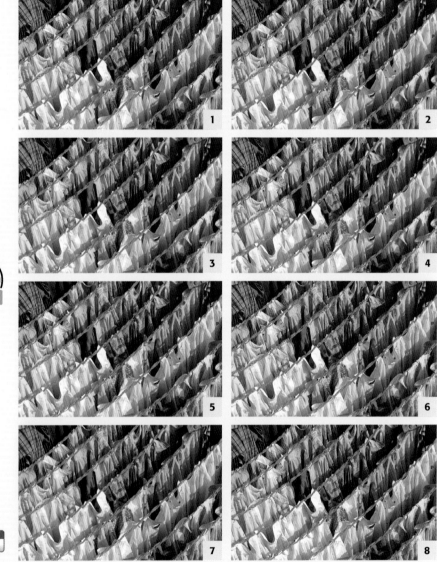

COMPLEX

I TOOK

MIN : SEC

SOLUTION ON PAGE 283

Up or down?

The Shanghai Pudong Airport is one of the busiest airports in the world.

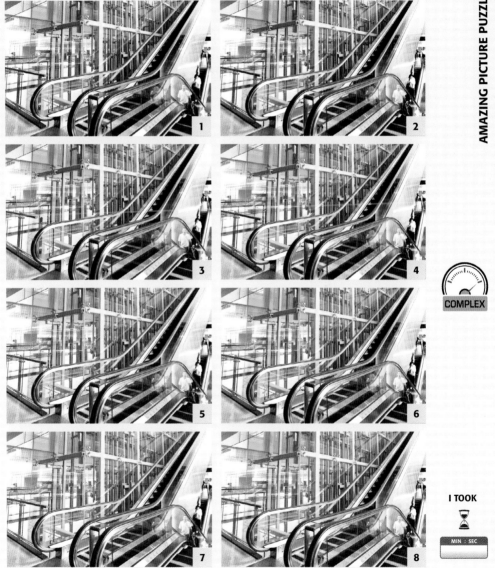

COMPLEX

I TOOK

MIN : SEC

SOLUTION ON PAGE 283

In a while, crocodile!

The most dangerous crocodiles are the Nile and the Australian crocodiles.

COMPLEX

I TOOK

MIN : SEC

THE DIFFERENCES I SPOTTED

SOLUTION ON PAGE 283

Uniqueness personified

"No one can possibly achieve any real and lasting success or 'get rich' in business by being a conformist." — J. Paul Getty

COMPLEX

I TOOK

MIN : SEC

THE DIFFERENCES I SPOTTED

08 ○○○○○○○○○

SOLUTION ON PAGE 283

Let me show you something

Can you spot all the differences between the two images?

COMPLEX

I TOOK

MIN : SEC

THE DIFFERENCES I SPOTTED

09 ○○○○○○○○○

SOLUTION ON PAGE 283

Party on!

As this band of girls paints the town red, try and find all the differences between the two images.

COMPLEX

I TOOK

MIN : SEC

THE DIFFERENCES I SPOTTED

07 ○○○○○○○

SOLUTION ON PAGE 284

Grandness personified

The Odeon of Herodes Atticus was built in AD 161 by
Herodes Atticus in memory of his wife, Aspasia Annia Regilla.

COMPLEX

I TOOK

MIN : SEC

THE DIFFERENCES I SPOTTED

07 ◐ ○○○○○○○

SOLUTION ON PAGE 284

Bicycle crazy!

Amsterdam is very popular for its cleanliness and environmentally friendly public bicycle system.

COMPLEX

I TOOK

MIN : SEC

THE DIFFERENCES I SPOTTED

06 ○○○○○○

SOLUTION ON PAGE 284

A pair of Pradas would be nice

While these cats get some shut-eye in the sun, try and find all the differences between these images.

COMPLEX

I TOOK

MIN : SEC

THE DIFFERENCES I SPOTTED

08 ○○○○○○○○

SOLUTION ON PAGE 284

Where are you all going?

While this baby elephant tries to convince his family to go swimming, see if you can spot all the differences between the two images.

COMPLEX

I TOOK

MIN : SEC

THE DIFFERENCES I SPOTTED

09

SOLUTION ON PAGE 284

The different faces of the corporate world

"You can't just ask customers what they want and then try and give it to them. By the time you get it built, they'll want something new."
— Steve Jobs

DID YOU KNOW?
Historically, it is believed that the first multinational company was the East India Company.

COMPLEX

I TOOK

MIN : SEC

THE DIFFERENCES I SPOTTED

10 ○○○○○○○○○○

SOLUTION ON PAGE 284

Flag fact

The current design of the American flag has been in use for more than fifty years. It was adopted in 1959.

COMPLEX

I TOOK

MIN : SEC

SOLUTION ON PAGE 285

My colorful ride

All these bicycles look alike, but there is an odd image.
Can you spot it?

COMPLEX

I TOOK

MIN : SEC

SOLUTION ON PAGE 285

It's your turn to find the ball

While these puppies search for the ball, try and look for all the differences between these two images.

COMPLEX

I TOOK

MIN : SEC

THE DIFFERENCES I SPOTTED

06 ○○○○○○

SOLUTION ON PAGE 285

Rush hour

Try and solve this puzzle before they reach the other side.

COMPLEX

I TOOK

MIN : SEC

THE DIFFERENCES I SPOTTED

09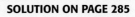

SOLUTION ON PAGE 285

Time is money

"Bizjet" is the colloquial term for a business jet or private jet.

COMPLEX

I TOOK

MIN : SEC

THE DIFFERENCES I SPOTTED

06 ⬦ ○○○○○○

SOLUTION ON PAGE 285

Thumbs up!

The gesture that in the West popularly denotes "well done" is considered an obscene gesture in Iran, Bangladesh, and Iran.

COMPLEX

I TOOK

MIN : SEC

THE DIFFERENCES I SPOTTED

06 ○○○○○○○

SOLUTION ON PAGE 285

Sun-kissed

To add to the fun, solve this puzzle with a loved one.

COMPLEX

I TOOK

MIN : SEC

THE DIFFERENCES I SPOTTED

07

SOLUTION ON PAGE 286

In health's honor

The Basilica of St. Mary of Health in Venice is commonly known as "Salute," which means "deliverance" in Italian.

COMPLEX

I TOOK

MIN : SEC

THE DIFFERENCES I SPOTTED

06 ○○○○○○

SOLUTION ON PAGE 286

Off to school!

Before this school of fish get to school, try and find all the differences between these two pictures.

COMPLEX

I TOOK

MIN : SEC

THE DIFFERENCES I SPOTTED

09

SOLUTION ON PAGE 286

Jumping jacks of the sea

In terms of diet, all dolphins are carnivores.

COMPLEX

I TOOK

MIN : SEC

THE DIFFERENCES I SPOTTED

06 ○○○○○○

SOLUTION ON PAGE 286

Wearing a mask is the most liberating feeling

The oldest masks that have been discovered are about 9,000 years old.

COMPLEX

I TOOK

MIN : SEC

SOLUTION ON PAGE 287

Dinnertime!
Everything is perfect but one image. Can you spot it?

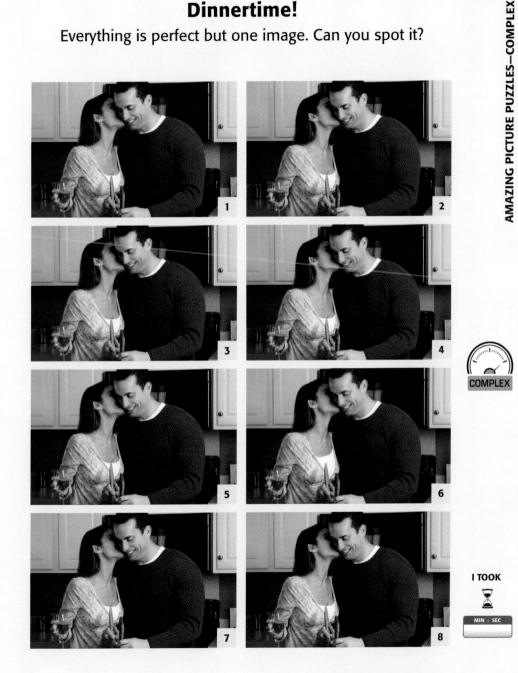

COMPLEX

I TOOK

MIN : SEC

SOLUTION ON PAGE 287

View from the top

Sydney Tower is the tallest structure in
Sydney, Australia.

DID YOU KNOW?
*Sydney Tower is also known as Centrepoint Tower.
It is 1,014 feet high and is a member of the
World Federation of Great Towers.*

COMPLEX

I TOOK

MIN : SEC

THE DIFFERENCES I SPOTTED

07 ○○○○○○○

SOLUTION ON PAGE 287

SOLUTIONS

SIMPLE

Page 9

Page 10

Page 11

Page 12

Page 13

Page 14

Page 15

Page 16

Page 17

Page 18

Page 21

Page 19

250

AMAZING PICTURE PUZZLES—SOLUTIONS

Page 22

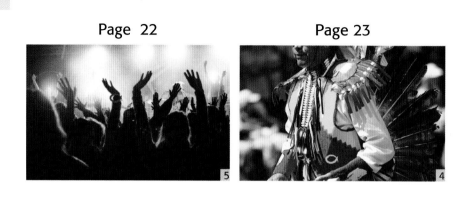

Page 23

Page 24

Page 25

Page 26

Page 27

Page 28

Page 29

Page 31

Page 32

Page 33

Page 34

Page 35

Page 36

Page 37

Page 38

Page 39

Page 40

Page 41

Page 42

Page 43

Page 44

Page 45

Page 47

Page 48

Page 49

Page 50

Page 51

Page 52

Page 53

Page 54

Page 55

Page 56

Page 57

Page 58

Page 59

Page 60

Page 61

Page 62

2

Page 63

4

Page 65

Page 66

3

Page 67

Page 68

Page 69

Page 70

Page 71

Page 72

Page 73

Page 74

Page 75

Page 76

Page 77

Page 78

Page 79

Page 80

Page 81

Page 82

Page 83

Page 84

Page 85

6

Page 87

SOLUTIONS

DIFFICULT

Page 91

Page 92

Page 93

Page 94

Page 95

Page 96

Page 97

Page 98

Page 99

Page 100

Page 101

Page 102

Page 103

Page 104

Page 105

Page 106

Page 109

Page 107

Page 110

Page 111

Page 112

Page 113

Page 114

Page 115

Page 116

Page 117

Page 118

Page 119

Page 120

Page 121

Page 123

Page 124

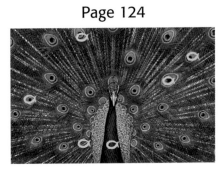

Page 125

Page 126

Page 127

Page 128

5

268

AMAZING PICTURE PUZZLES—SOLUTIONS

Page 129

Page 130

Page 131

Page 132

Page 133

Page 134

Page 135

Page 136

Page 137

Page 138

Page 139

Page 140

Page 141

Page 142

Page 143

Page 144

Page 145

Page 146

Page 147

Page 148

Page 149

Page 151

Page 152

Page 153

Page 154

Page 155

Page 156

Page 157

Page 158

Page 159

Page 160

Page 161

Page 162

Page 163

Page 164

Page 165

Page 166

Page 167

Page 168

Page 169

Page 171

Page 175

Page 176

Page 177

Page 178

Page 179

Page 180

Page 181

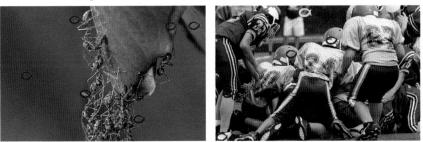

Page 182

Page 183

Page 184

Page 185

Page 186

Page 187

Page 188

Page 189

Page 190

Page 191

Page 192

Page 193

Page 194

Page 195

Page 197

Page 198

Page 199

Page 200

Page 201

Page 202

Page 203

Page 204

Page 205

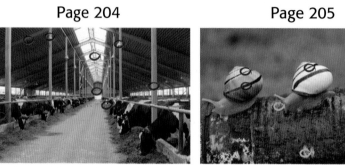

Page 206

Page 207

Page 209

Page 210

Page 211

Page 212

Page 213

Page 214

Page 215

Page 216

Page 217

Page 218

Page 219

Page 220

Page 221

Page 222

Page 223

Page 224

Page 225

Page 226

Page 227

Page 228

Page 229

Page 231

Page 232

Page 233

Page 234

Page 235

Page 236

Page 237

Page 238

Page 239

Page 240

Page 241

Page 242

Page 243

Page 245